Blessings In The Storm

Samuel Wesley Gathing: A Closer Look

Roberta Wright

Printed in the United States of America.

ISBN: 978-1-4269-3770-5 (sc)
ISBN: 978-1-4269-3771-2 (e)

Trafford rev. 04/27/2011

Trafford
PUBLISHING® www.trafford.com

North America & international
toll-free: 1 888 232 4444 (USA & Canada)
phone: 250 383 6864 ♦ fax: 812 355 4082

In Memory of
Sam & Beatrice
Who never stopped praying for their children

ACKNOWLEDGEMENTS

This book was born from conversations with my brothers and sisters. My sister Cozetta was the first to suggest I do a family tree of our father. I am grateful for my brothers and sisters for their memories of years gone past. Without Sam Jr., Obadiah, Cozetta, Ruth, Lloyd, James, Alberta, Betty, and Laura this book would not have been written.

A special thanks to my single daughter, Pamela, a working mother of two who took the time out of her busy schedule and did the copy and editing which kept this book on track.

DEDICATION

This book is dedicated to my daughter, Pamela, grandson, Ronelle, granddaughter, Tamela and my sister Cozetta.

TABLE OF CONTENTS

PREFACE

This book is about Sam and Beatrice struggle raising their children in the midst of the Jim Crow Laws where their children were viewed as stupid nigger kids and the system that enforce that view.

In this era of Jim Crow, Sam had to maneuver his way through a maze of irrational hatred of landmines that was placed before his steps to destroy him and his family.

Samuel Wesley Gathing
A Closer Look; the
Husband, The Father,
The Man
Poppa

Born in 1908, 2nd of 2 children of John Wesley and Cynthia Gathing, Sam Wesley Gathing entered the world on April 25, 1908 in a small rural town in northern Mississippi and also into an environment of bitter hatred and hostility from the southern whites. His father was a farmer who owned 5 acres of land and grew his own tobacco. The boy learned early the importance of hard work and saving money. His mother, Cynthia died when he was 6 months old probably complication from childbirth.

This journey was chartered and documented in collaboration with generations of information.

Chapter 1 - Searching For An Answer

Sam left Mississippi when he was 18 years old to find work in Madison, IL. While living with his Uncle Luscher, Sam found employment in a Steel Mill. The young man saved every penny that he could because he had made up his mind that he would return back to Mississippi when he had enough money saved to marry his childhood sweetheart, Beatrice. December 22, 1929, in the state of Mississippi; Desoto County, Sam and Beatrice became husband and wife.

For a wedding gift Sam's father gave him a mule name "Rock" and a big red cow. Sam bred this red cow and over the years her offspring's produced over 75 cattle and calves.

Sam, like other people of his era, has seen triumphs and tragedies. He has witness wars, revolutions and social upheavals.

Sam and Beatrice moved several times as their young family grew. They leased land from white land owners. It was rare during the 1930's and 40's that Negroes in the south were land owners. So Sam and his wife had to tolerate racist land owners to lease their land.

Rent was paid in hard labor from the cotton Sam and his young family produced. Rent for the Martin Place – 3 bales of cotton.

Sam rented 300 acres from the Nicholas place and the young man paid 13 bails of cotton per year in rent. Sometimes these leases would last for 4 years.

With his leased land, he was allowed to sublease to other farmers. The farmers were called "share croppers." Share Cropper: A person who farms land owned by another and get's part of the crop in return for the use of the leased land.

He rented several different farms over the years because often some conflict would arrive with him and the racist land owner.

In today's climate, it is hard to imagine the life that Sam was forced to live.

For this young man was born to be a leader. In the presence of Sam, you could sense his power to influence and persuade.

However, with his strong character around white people, Sam had to play the roll of a boy around white men, women and their children also. I am sure the whites could see his strength. The racist whites knew he was not stupid. But under the Jim Crow Laws, this outrageous roll was played for years. The Negro man was not allowed to look or make eye contact with a white man. Negro men could not work on the same job with a White man. The Black Man of any Black person could not drink, eat or sit where whites did.

Throughout this period it was acceptable for whites to call any Black person "nigger". Nigger this! Nigger that! By calling our Poppa boy and Nigger, they were using the worst possible slurs. It was a daily struggle for Sam to keep his heart from being contaminated with the spirit of hate. It was hard for his children to witness their strong intelligent Poppa pretending before white folks that he was inferior to them. When talking to whites with down casted eyes, because blacks wasn't allowed to make eye contact with whites, saying "Ya'som or no-som and hearing whites calling our father "boy".

This experience his children witness built up resentment against the whites and what they stood for.

Over time this resentment became a deep and bitter anger that eventually weaken or destroyed their playful childhood spirit. Is part of the story. Even in their old age their playful childhood attitude about life wasn't restored. This lost of joy in their lives makes us all understand why Jesus said to forgive your "enemies".

Most of his children saw the Jesus that their Poppa preached about as a unloving white man that was related to the evil white men because the Jesus that they saw looked like a white man with white skin and straight silky hair. How can this Jesus be a friend to these evil white men and be a friend to the black man too? They asked.

On a daily bases the opposition from the whites grew worst as Sam boys got older. White males saw them as a bigger threat to the southern white authority.

This resentment Rev Gathing boys felt entangled them into a web of rage and hatred.

During this time in American history there were many militant voices on the public stage that were screaming that they were angry also. These voices of Malcolm X, Stokely Carmichael, the Black Panther, Elijah Mohammed were very angry black man, among others, that said with a loud convincing voice that they had the answer for the American blacks.

Some of Rev Gathing boys were persuaded that these angry black men had the answer they needed. They turned their back on the God of their father. They forsaken the ancient faith and turned their attention to Elijah Mohammed and Islam.

Jer 6:16 – stand at the cross road and look, ask for the ancient path.

It would appear, so at least for a time, that the high uplifted arm with a tightly clenched fist while screaming "Black Power"! Black Power! We want it now was also the answer – years past and we all found out that it would take more, much more than that to rise to the educational and economical level that other races appear to reach with ease.

Why are these accomplishment so easy for other and so difficult for blacks?

Unthankfulness. Not taking advantage of all the opportunities placed in front of us. Could this be so? It's not clear, but one thing is clear, too many are not thankful.

In Sam's home and around other blacks when no whites were present, illustrated the thrusting growth of the man – his evolution, rapid growth toward the man he might have been if his intelligence hadn't ran into resistance from the southern whites

There is, however, an inevitability built into the natural order of things – cause and effect are in fact joined. When people whole lives is lived in the midst of hatred and obstacles it is natural for resentment to build. For rage to take hold And take hold it did.

Sam had a yearning for more. Although Sam had to play this roll around whites he took being a man very serious, this negro man knew what a man was suppose to be like God told him. For Sam read his bible daily. He believed what God said about man not what the southern whites said. Sam's children heard him say many times, "when I was a child, I thought like a child, I reasoned like a child. When I became a man, I put childish ways behind me." 1 Cor. 13:11.

The American Negro men, women and their children had spent their entire lives in American harshest environment imaginable. In 1857 the US Supreme Court decision in the case of Dred Scott that no black could be a US Citizen and that black people had no rights in America that white people were bound to respect (p178) before the Mayflower by Lerone Bennett, Jr. A Negro Spiritual:

I am going through; yes I'll pay the price No matter what others do, Yes, I'll take the way on the Lord's battle field I started in Jesus and I am going through....

5

Gal. 5:1 (NIV)

It is for freedom that Christ has set us free, stand firm, then, and do not let yourselves be burned again by a yoke of slavery.

Psalm 1:3 (NIV)

*He is like a tree planted by streams of water which yields its fruit in season and whose leaf does not wither whatever he does prosper.

These Negros knew that power concedes nothing without demands and they had to challenge power with truth.

Amazing how this may sound this environment did not weaken their spirit. This horrific experience built up their courage and determination. Even though it was a law that a black man had no rights that a white man had to obey, with this law always hanging over the black's head and with the odds stacked against them this drove the Negroes to pursue answers beyond their own realm.

Just to name a few great Negro men and women who vision wasn't limited to their own time and experience:

W.E.B. Dubois, Martin L. King Jr., Thurgood Marshall, Frederick Douglas, Jesse Jackson, Medgar Evers, Booker T. Washington. Women: Fannie Lou Hammer, Coretta Scott King, Harriet Tubman, Mary McLeod Bethune, Sojourner Truth.

Chapter 2 - Down on the Farm

The morning sun hadn't risen yet. The sounds of the night could be heard. Sam's older boys, Sam Jr. Obadiah and young Alfred were milking cows. A pail, short stool, two hands and a very gentle cow are all they needed to enjoy fresh milk every day.

Sam sold the milk from his boys' labor to increase his much needed income to $100.00 per month during the 40's depression.

It was also the boys' responsibility to make sure the milk did not spoil before the milkman came around before the boys went to school to pick-up the milk cans. They did this by putting the full milk cans in cold water – this was before the refrigerator. Sam Jr., Obadiah and young Alfred took turns getting up through the night to change the water around the milk cans to make sure the water stayed cold because if the milk was spoil when the milkman got it to the cheese processing plant the milkman would return the spoil milk back to Sam.

Milking cows were only one of Sam's boys job. There were many others like cutting wood, feeding the farm animals, sometimes hunting for rabbits or squirrels for our next meal, etc. For these were boys' jobs. Girls didn't do these things because there was a very clear line drawn that separated what girls did and what boys did.

The older girls assisted their mother and the boys assisted their father. The older children also assisted in the rearing of their younger sisters and brothers. For the younger siblings knew that their older siblings were their second parent.

Most of the early years for Sam and his family were lived in a traditional framed house with a tin roof with no indoor plumbing. Despite this fact, Sam and Beatrice's children loved to hear rhythm of the rain beating against the roof top. It was soothing and comforting to hear the rain drops tapping on the tin roof, as our father sometimes told us stories or as we slept through the night.

With the invention of the light bulb in the late 1800's people lives changed.

Most people didn't believe it … they couldn't figure it out in their minds. It was sort of like when the first air plane were built or when man went to the moon. Poor uneducated people couldn't comprehend, with a snap of a switch light would enter their homes – only lighting they had ever known was oil, candles or kerosene. Why this "light bulb" thing sounded like magic. Do you believe that? I'er believe it when I see it or Naw', Lord I sure don't." Were some of the comment of the times.

However, it was true. And in the late 40's the Gathing household received indoor lighting.

We, like other children, didn't enjoy going to the fields to work so the rain made us happy knowing that it would be too wet to work in the field the next day.

These traditional framed houses were cold in the winter with maybe one wood burning fireplace. The desire to keep her family warm kept our mother and other mothers of that era very busy making quilts from old cloths by cutting out small pieces of fabric from them and stitching them by hand together. When this work was finished it would form a beautiful tapestry work of art.

Sometimes women would get together to make quilts.

They laughed and talked like women do today – about their men and children.

When the weather turned warm every one was anxious to get outside out of the heat indoors. Sam and Beatrice would sit in their favorite chair on the front porch as they watched their children playing barefoot in the dust, singing nursery rhymes.

Maybe four or five of their daughters would make a large circle as they held hands while one of the girls would be squatting in the center. Round and round they would go as they sing to the girl squatting in the center. Round and round they would go as they sing to the squatting girl and dust flying as the girl's bare feet hit the earth….

Little Sally Walker
Sitting in a saucer
Rise, Sally Rise-
Put your hands on your hips and let your back bone slip.
Shake it to the east,
Shake it to the west,
Shake it to the one that you love the best.
Your Momma said so
Your Poppa said so
That's the way to shake it if you want to catch your Bow.

The girls had their street rhymes and the boys had their also. "Hambone" was one of the boys' favorite. The boy would lean forward as he sits on a chair with one hand hitting his lower thigh while still leaning, he would hit his lips with a popping sound while singing…

Hambone, Hambone, where you been?
Round the world and back again
Hambone, Hambone, where's your wife?
She's in the kitchen cooking rice.
Hambone, Hambone, have you heard?
Poppa gonna buy me a mocking bird.
If that mocking bird don't sing,
Poppa gonna buy me a diamond ring.
If that diamond ring turns brass
Poppa gonna buy me a looking glass.
If that looking glass gets broke
Poppa gonna buy me a billy goat.
Hambone, Hambone!

Jump rope, hide and go seek, checkers, jack rocks, and there were other games. Sam's children played many games.

Our Poppa didn't get his first television until the early fifties and even after getting it, T.V. only had 3 channels and it wasn't aired all night. Their children had a lot of leisure time and used it for fun and games.

Sam mostly cultivated cotton, corn and garden vegetables and other kinds of root vegetables. All hands were required in the fields. Our lives revolved around the cycle of plowing, planting and harvesting. So at a young age, we children were called into action helping our parents.

When the field work was done, Sam and Beatrice's' children had lots of play time. We played Cowboys and Indians, B.B. Guns and Cap Pistols were considered toys to play with. The girls played in a home-made playhouse outside where we had tea parties with the tea set we got for Christmas. For these were the days of "The Long Ranger", "Hop-Along Cassidy", "Roy Rogers and Del Even". The games we played were influenced by these T.V. programs.

At night, because we were many miles from the city lights, we got the full effects of the nights. As we played outside, the lights from the moon alone, we could see our shadows and many falling stars.

Children started going to the fields at a young age of 6 or 7 years old. Sam young children were given a Crocker Sack for the cotton they picked. The small sacks were once used for corn seed; however, thought the word "recycle" wasn't part of Sam and Beatrice vocabulary. They only saw what could be reused. In today's climate recycling is encouraged to protect the environment. For Beatrice, it was to keep the cost of the running of her household down. With many mouths to feed, this was important.

Flour that came in printed cloth sacks, our mother made us gowns or underwear. With store bought can goods or jars, when empty, and after thoroughly washing, these were reused for drinking containers.

The older children had 6ft. sacks for picking cotton. When these sacks were full of cotton, they would hold 100lbs of cotton or more.

While working in the fields, side by side, singing, telling jokes, sharing secrets, the bonding between Sam and Beatrice's' children grew and at night the girls shared bedrooms and the boys shared a room too which pulled the knots of their bonding even tighter.

Before the sun rose, we could smell the aroma of coffee and out mother frying sausages or port fat back. We knew our mother would be calling us to breakfast.

While they were eating, Jesus took bread, gave thanks and broke it. (Mat. 26:26) For no one could start eating until we were all at the table.

For Beatrice and Sam thought it was ungodly – even a sin to start eating before He, the head of his house, hadn't blessed the table. So at the call of "BREAKFAST!" from our dear mother, was not an option to not be at the table.

No one ate a crumb before Poppa or before Poppa blessed the table. With all heads bowed and as home-made biscuits, eggs, rice and sometime a special treat of hot chocolate milk awaits our hungry stomachs.

Our father would bless our food:
Gracious Lord,
Thank Thee for the food we are 'bout to receive
And the nursing our bodies,
For Christ sake —
Amen!

…then our mother:
Blessed is the mercy
For they shall obtain mercy-
Amen!

As we stayed standing around this large round table, Beatrice and Sam's children said their Bible verses one by one before we could all eat.

Exodus 20:8-10 (NIV)

Remember the Sabbath day by keeping it Holy.

Six days you shall labor and do all your work, But the seventh day is a Sabbath to the Lord, Your God.

On it, you shall not do any work, Neither you, nor your son or daughter, nor your manservant or maidservant, nor your animals, nor the alien within your gates.

Beatrice told her children don't sew on this day of Holiness for sewing on this day is like putting needles through Jesus.

Our father and mother told us many things like parents do today to get their children's attention. However, everything stopped on Sunday except cooking, eating and going to church.

After a long week of going to school, many chores, assisting our parents indoors and outdoors, it was easy for us to except this reality that everything came to a squeaking halt on Sunday.

Compared to early T.V. with only 3 channels and during this time, T.V. was not aired all night like today. Man and woman were not allowed to share the same bed. Kissing was allowed, thought. If Poppa walked in the room and saw his children watching a white man and woman (Blacks wasn't allowed to kiss in public), kissing, we knew as children we were caught red-handed – Opps! Poppa caught us watching this trash, "cut that junk off now! How dare you watch these white folks lapping themselves in the mouth"! So, one of his children would rush to the television and cut it off – this was before the remote control.

It is to be observed, too, that the Negro man and his family were saddled with a lot of societal problems; however, in their own world, there were lots of good in those years of darkness.

Men showed women respect by never using offensive language around them. When a woman entered the room, men and children would stand and offer their seats. They also open doors for her. When walking past a women, men would tip their hats, "howdy ma'am". Men paid the bills.

In return, woman serviced man by cooking for them, cleaning, washing, ironing for their man, making sure their man was dressed for the occasion. These etiquettes of the times were rarely broken.

Over the years, Sam and Beatrice owned 8 mules and horses; Rock, Shorty, Ida, Ole Mike, Lucy, Scott, Beauty and Twilight were their names. In these early years before machinery, animals and man needed each other. Animals were rarely thought of as pets. In these times, farmers had an intimate relationship with their animals. They would call them by name and sometimes Sam's children could hear them talking about his animals as though they were one of his children. "Beauty" did this or "Twilight" is acting like she is sick or some cow got out; a fox raided the chicken coop and got all the eggs.

The weather was a constant worry. Our father would say, "Lord, we need rain", or "Lord, we need it to stop raining".

Sometimes Sam would look up at the late evening sky, just before the sun went down and if a cloud is covering the sun, he would know it would rain the next day.

You see, with a farmer, everything depends on the weather.

To have a healthy crop, the weather has to be right.

This young Negro man had many worries. His churches, his children, his animals, his finances – always wondering will there be enough? So after the rain had stopped and Sam looked up and saw a rainbow in the sky, he knew there would be no rain the next day. For God had put the rainbow there for a warning to man, "…no more rain but fire next time…". 1948 was a turning point for Sam's life because he bought his first tractor. After he and his boys walked behind horses and mules for years plowing. Thank God, for Sam actually owned a tractor!

Sam was always on the cutting edge of life. He paid close attention to world events. This awareness pulled this young man forward out of the shadows of "poor me", "I can't", "it's their fault". So when he heard about the invention of the automobile, "Great Stars!" was one of his saying when he was excited. He knew he was going to own one someday.

After returning from Madison, IL., and before marrying his pretty young bride, Sam bought his first automobile – a model "A" Ford for $250.00. As the years past, there were many other cars:

1929 Model "T" Ford
1934 Ford
1937 Ford
1938 Chevy…and the list continued.

Like the years before the 1940's, where difficult times. The years of midwives, no electricity, before indoor plumbing, child birth death wasn't uncommon. There were many highly contagious childhood diseases: Polio, Whooping Cough, Scarlett Fever, Diphtheria and Yellow Fever and there were others. Many vaccinations were yet to come and then there was the Great Depression.

Sam said doing this time poor people saw very little money, if any. He told his children during the depression, he only saw .30 cent in one year. However, with God's help and the animals God gave man to assist him, man survived. Food was scarce. Beatrice's' children could hear her praying, "Lord, have mercy on us".

In 1960 – 1965, mad cow disease killed most of his cattle. He and Beatrice were discouraged. However, they did not give up hope on the lost of most of their cattle. For they had faced many tough times before – maybe this scripture came to Sam.

2 Cor. 4:16 (NIV)

Therefore we do not lose heart though outwardly we are wasting Away, yet inwardly, we are being renewed day by day.

So with prayer and hope, he put his old muddy boots on and starting breeding his cattle again.

Chapter 3 - A Time to Preach

Samuel Wesley Gathing

Sam said he knew at age 9 after receiving Christ, that he was called to preach.

"Oh what joy came over my soul since I met Jesus".

1 Cor 3:7

So neither he who plants, nor he who waters is anything, but only God who makes thing grows.

This young Negro boy grew with the spiritual seed God planted in him at age 9 to pastor several churches and preached for 42 years. Sam also was a moderator for Sardis East Baptist BTU Congress and assisted Evergreen Usher Confederation.

As moderator, Rev. Gathing held the gravel seeking ways also to solve internal disputes these churches encountered.

Sardis East Congress was a conglomerate of churches that spread throughout several adjacent counties in northern Mississippi.

During the 1800's - 1950's, these churches pooled their money in an organized way to build schools for their children.

This was also a time in black American history that black males were organizing. The Sardis East Baptist (1887), The NAACP (1909), Negro College Fund or UNCF (1943), just a few that reflected this.

The black males in the hostile environment of the Jim Crow Laws overcame many challenges exercising their God given strength.

They worked around the barriers that were placed before them - these men working through the obstacles brought unity.

Rev. Gathing faced his task as a moderator the same ways he faces his churches - with confidence, for he was accustom to standing before large audience which kindled a love in him for public speaking.

His medium frame of approximately 5'6" and 165 lbs was easy for him to handle as he walked with urgency as though he was rushing to this place so he could get to the next place.

When walking with Poppa, it took effort to keep up.

I don't think men ever left their homes without their hats.

Poppa was no different with his old gray or black hat pulled low on his head, walking swiftly in the cool fall wind to check on his live stock. His children often heard him talking to himself. Poppa had so much within.

In these modern times, we take for granted on-scheduled pay days. We know exactly the amount of money we are going to receive. We can count on it. Not so with farmers. In Sam's era, they did not know how much money they were going to receive for their labor. With farmers, it was all about the weather. If it did not rain enough, it damaged the crop. If it rain too much, it damaged the crop. Even the insects played a roll in their worries. Insects like bow weavers invaded the cotton crop and sometimes Locus. Some type of worms invaded the corn. Every plant had their own enemies.

For Sam to keep his churches running, he had to hope his members had a giving spirit. This young man 14 children is a whole book in itself.

He was very charismatic which causes him to demonstrate an exceptional ability for leadership and securing the devotion of large number of people. Is it any wonder he talked to himself and God often?

Before He left for church on Sunday, Beatrice would do a full military inspection of her husband, starting at the top of his head, tying his tie & making sure it was straight, checking his hair, his mustache, his full front view, down to his shoes, making sure there was no lint on his dark suit or dirt on his shoes. Then she would have her husband turn slowly around and do a full review inspection. When our mother has finished her inspection knowing now that her husband is ready for church. Beatrice knew that all eyes on the sanctuary would be on her husband as he stands at the podium to preach.

When Sam walked out the front door to go to church, he felt confident because he knew "Brassy", that's what he called Beatrice, always did her inspections well.

Before Rev. Gathing would start to preach, the church choir would sing:

> ...I'm going through;
> I'll pay the price no matter what others do
> I'll take the way that the lord told me to do.
> I'm going through,
> I'll take the way I started in Jesus and I'm going through
> Yes, I'll pay the price no matter what others do...

And as Rev. Gathing rose out of his Pastor's chair walking toward the podium with his old Bible in his hand. All eyes in the sanctuary are upon him as he started to preach.

Rev. Gathing preached about the Lord's Supper. A sermon he preached always, like other churches, on First Sunday.

Our father is reading from Mat. 26:26-29:

"While they were eating, Jesus took bread, gave thanks and broke it, and gave it to his disciples, saying," Take and eat; this is my body." Then he took the cup, gave thanks and offered it to them saying, "Drink from it, all of you. This is my blood of the covenant, which is poured out for many for the forgiveness of sin.29 I tell you, I will not drink of this fruit of the vine from now on until that day when I drink it a new with you in my Father's kingdom."

Rev. Gathing continued preaching, saying, "Christian people are supposed to meet on the Sabbath Day and we are meeting all over this land. All those who love the Lord should be at some church on Sunday. We are grateful today to have as many present today as we do. Sometimes we put too much emphasis on "Easter". Every Sunday should be treated like "Easter" Sunday.

Christ went to the temple when he was 12 years old. For 21 years, Christ celebrated the feast of the past over. The feast was the remembering of a greater feast. It was a type of feast for yet to come, "the feast of the communion". Christ did not give us how often we should do communion, he just said in remembering of HIM.

There was a certain man who went to the temple to pray.

One man was telling God how good he was. Another man just said Lord have mercy on me, a sinner. You never get too good; there is always room for improvement. If we listen closely to Christ teaching, we will get the TRUTH. When your time comes to die, you know what is going to save you…the grace of God. We try to tell people what is going to save them. The truth is going to save them and Jesus is the truth.

As Sam popularity grew more and more demands were made on this gifted Negro man. More churches wanted him for their Pastor.

Rev. Gathing was now the pastor of two churches, Ebenezer and St. Joseph. Sam was only in his late 30's.

Everything was moving fast for him now. The years of the mid 40's and through the 1950's. His family was constantly growing. Through all of this, God sent him a mentor, an old Negro preacher by the name of Rev. Roger Person.

Sam knew that he did not know how, as a young preacher, to handle all the growing demands that were being made upon him. Poppa was wise enough to know this.

Poppa trusted this old Negro preacher. For Sam appreciated Rev. Person's experiences. God had also given him Sam and old man Person an example in the Bible to live by because they both read their Bible daily. This old man and his young man had read many times in 1 Timothy and 2 Timothy how the apostle Paul gave young Timothy advice.

Rev. Person knew Sam would face all sorts of pressures, conflicts and challenges from the church and surrounding culture.

Like Apostle Paul, who gave Timothy fatherly advice, warning Timothy about false teachers and urging him to hold on to his faith in Christ. Roger Person gave the young Minister Sam the same advice.

In the twentieth century American history of poverty begins with most working people living on the edge of destitution, periodically short of food, fuel, clothing and shelter. Poverty was wide spread through the 1940's, 1950's and beyond.

Farmers who income was poor could grow much of the food needed to feed their families. Through the Great Depression, most farmers remained poor. In 1950 two-thirds of the farmers lived in poverty. Children often contributed significantly to family income. Sometimes Sam would loan his children out to work for other farmers and part of the money children earned would help support the family. On the average, each child was paid $3.00 per day for chopping or picking cotton.

During the 1940's and 50's gas prices was .20 cent per gallon or less. So $3.00 per child made a difference and was very helpful for the family income.

About ten miles from the small town of Byhalia, MS, a town like other towns in the south, where in the 50's you could see, feel and smell the affect of Jim Crow Laws. The signs of separation were out in the open. The superior of the whites were screamed out loud. "No Colored Allowed" signs were all over the place.

When a white policeman pulled a Negro over, the Negro tremble with fear because he knew that Negros had no rights that a white person had to respect.

This ten mile drive was not an easy drive. This drive was a drive on the primitive dirt road. When it would rain you could not get in your car or truck and drive on it you had to wait sometime for the rain to stop because so many mud holes you may get stuck. Sometimes the hard rain washed part of the road away. Dirt roads came before gravel.

During the ten miles drive, you would occasionally pass a "Victorian-era house". A veranda that wraps around the front and sides of the vastly huge house that had all the reminders of slavery with wooden framed shacks near by that poor Negros lived in as they worked for their ex-slave master.

The black community had started talking about this young preacher named Rev. Gathing. The white community whispered about this Negro man. Black and white, when they heard the name Sam Gathing, their ears perked up. Rev. Gathing had become the Pastor of his third church.

This was the era of traveling evangelist. Black and white ministers would travel from town, city or state preaching and giving revival services. Sometimes the preacher and their members would have service in an open field or tent.

So for Sam to have more than one church showed his popularity. He would preach on 1st Sunday at one church, 2nd Sunday at another church, etc. Mt. Sinai was the third church Rev. Gathing would pastor.

Our Poppa had a large view of the world. He talked a lot about travel. Maybe even someday going to Israel, where Jesus walked. He didn't go though. 1945 under these conditions of poverty and Jim Crow Laws, Sam became the pastor of an old dilapidated framed church that was built in 1884. The first structure was destroyed by fire and rebuilt in 1893.

Our mother said that when he started pastoring this church, tin buckets were set inside the church to catch the water that leaked from the tin leaky roof. Two by fours were propped against the old wooden frame to keep the church from falling.

Beatrice was really worried. Did Sam know what he was doing? Did her husband realize what he was getting his family into? The roads were horrible, there were no stores near by, no doctors "back yonder". This church was so far from everything.

Beatrice felt a since of her husband pulling her and her children into the unknown. Why he was even talking about buying land and moving "back yonder" away from her immediate family.

Beatrice world was small. It was surrounded by her family, her mother, father and her nine sisters and brothers and, of course, her husband and her children.

Beatrice did not have a desire to know anything else.

This pretty young woman, about 5'4", with light brown complexion and shoulder length hair, felt complete in her own world. Laughter came easy for her; unlike her husband, she didn't have a yearning for more. However; like her husband she read her Bible daily also. Beatrice believed that the man was the head of his household.

Eph 5:22-24:
Wives, submit to your husbands as to the Lord.
For the husband is the head of the wife as Christ is the head of the church, his body of which he is the Savior.

Eph. 5:25:
Husbands, love your wives, just as Christ loved the church And gave himself up for her.

Jesus to His disciples.

Mat. 10:11-13:
Whatever town or village you enter, search for some worthy person there and stay at his house until you leave.
As you enter the home, give it your greeting. If the home is deserving, let your peace rest on it; if it is not, let your peace return to you."

Chapter 4 - Alone with Momma

When travelling to one of his distance churches, Poppa would leave on most weekends to talk with his Deacons or have some type of meeting before church service on Sunday.

These meetings were done on Saturday and Poppa would spend most of Saturday meeting and preparing for Sunday's church service. Rev. Gathing would spend Saturday with one of his church members' home. This was done mostly before telephones. To communicate, people had to meet face to face.

(l-r: Alfred, Obadiah, James, Lloyd and Sam Jr.)

Sam's children loved it. We had Momma all to ourselves.

Our mother was so easy to be around. Laughter came easy for her. With Momma, you could sometimes bend the rules – not so with Poppa. When Poppa said, "I brought you in this world and I could take you out of this world", we believed him – not so with Momma. We would laugh if Momma said that.

(l-r: Cynthia, Cozetta, Ruth, Christine, Iola, Alberta, Roberta, Betty Jo and Peggy)

Poppa didn't believe in playing with children. He knew that the line was too thin and it would be too easy for one of his children to disrespect him once the parent open the door for child's play behavior. On some weekends, our Poppa would buy us a special treat of soda pop, bologna, cheese and crackers and cookies. This showed his tenderness despite his strict discipline which he kept within narrow and specific limits, enforcing and maintaining strict standards.

When Poppa left for these weekend trips, we felt a sense of freedom. Why sometimes some of Sam's children would actually have the pleasure of sleeping with their mother.

Momma was there when we came home from school, form working in the fields; Momma was always there for her children. Momma was a symbol of gentleness, love and peace.

When one of Beatrice children needed to be punished, she believed "to spare the rod, spoil the child". When momma whipped one of us, she would often say, "This hurts me more than it hurts you." Momma never left us, we left her. Beatrice's children heard her say, "I know my children had to leave, that's what grown children do, but it's so hard not hearing the commotion of my children running through the house."

Beatrice had never been away from her children before, never!

Momma had never been alone. Sam was gone a lot doing what he'd always did – dealing with church matters. Beatrice felt so alone "down yonder" by herself. The stillness, the echo of silence at times was more than our mother could bear. The silence overwhelmed her. She wept.

In these modern times of 2009, a distance of ten or twenty miles doesn't seem far. However; though, when the roads were bad and most poor people did not have telephones, all communications were done face to face or by mail. To know this helps us understand our mother's concerns. Sam and his wife always lived near Olive Branch, MS or Byhalia, MS area. Momma didn't know anyone "back yonder".

In later years when Beatrice and Sam's children migrated up north for there were no jobs for Negros down south.

When their children talked it was mostly about their parents "down yonder". Especially their mother. What can we get for Momma? Does Momma need anything? How about Poppa?

Lets buy Momma this or Poppa that. Sam's children found much joy in their spirit finally being able to buy for their parents "down yonder". Our thoughts were often with them and his children went "down yonder" to visit often.

After pastoring Mt. Sinai for 1 year, Rev. Gathing thought "Ah! I think I'm going to rebuild this church. This building is in horrible shape".

As Rev. Gathing brought his idea to the Deacons, what did they think? For this was thought of before, but never done. Did the "Nay Sayers" come forward with their doubts?

Did they say it can't be done? How are you going to get this kind of money from all these poor people?

Rev. Gathing had some doubts himself; however, though when he read his Bible and God's word told him how Solomon in 1 Kinds 3:9 asked God for wisdom and a discerning heart.

Reading this, Sam knew that wisdom is only effective when it is put into action! The Bible says in 1 King 5 that God sent Solomon all the help he needed to build the temple for God.

So Rev. Gathing stepped on the word of God in faith. The 2nd "corner stone" was laid in 1946.

His churches were a big part of his life, probably the biggest part. His conversation was mostly about his churches and his members. Our Poppa loved them.

Chapter 5 - The Picture

It was a climate of rising hope and rising despair. A mother that Sam had often heard about but did not know that the memories about his mother are always the reel playing in his head. "Get over it" the voice in his head kept saying. But he can't. So many things cause his mother to come to mind.

A mother that he heard about but did not know.

For it was 1949, Sam was 41 years old before someone gave him an old worn, black and white picture with cracked lines from aging of his mother. Sam held this picture, feeling like a small child again, with tears in his eyes as he stared at seeing the image of his mother he had never seen. A mother who his oldest child was named after, "Cynthia". So, this is her. "Why", Sam said in almost inaudible whisper, "Cozetta" looks like her (Cozetta is Poppa's third child).

This woman, my mother who gave birth to me and died because of it, who loved and nursed me for 6 months before dying.

As Rev. Gathing set in his pastor's chair in the pulpit on Mother's Day, some people in the church wearing a white carnation which signifies that their mothers were deceased and others wore a red carnation signifying that their mothers were living.

Rev. Gathing is listening to this song & no matter how hard he tries in his spirit it always hurt to hear it.....

I've got a mother gone home
Oh I've got a mother gone home
Yes I want to go to glory
Yes I want to surely see her there
Yes I want to meet her there
Once I had a mother who talked to me
Oh death has called her to heaven
Her face one day I'll see
She said death has come to my door

Child I really had to go
I hate to leave you here in this world below
I want to go to heaven
I want to meet her there

Chapter 6 - A Time to Celebrate

The Harvesting season was finally over. The long, hot, dusty summer days has ended. It is time to put away our cotton sacks; set aside out water jugs we had to drench our thirst as we worked in the dry heat. It was time to hang up our loved straw hats. The hats that Sam's children had grown to love because our straw hats were the only thing we had to separate us from the awful heat of Mississippi sun while working in the fields.

At the end of planting season in June and the end of harvesting season in late October, Sam and Beatrice always took their children shopping for spring and fall clothes. We were all excited for at the end of harvesting season. Poppa always celebrated with his family by taking them about forty miles to Memphis's State Fair.

Like sardines packed in a can, Sam packed his kids in his car or truck, with brand new clothes, brand new shoes, feeling good and looking new. This song comes to mind, *"Don't you step on my blue suede shoes"*.

With his children heart filled with great expectations of amusement, cotton candy, soda pop, popcorn, etc., Sam is speeding toward Byhalia, MS about ten miles from where we lived. He drove through this small town on the way to Memphis and as Poppa approaches this small town, there's a steep hill. Before our Poppa get to this hill, he would press down on the gas peddle and climb this steep hill as fast as he possibly could. When his car reaches the top, it felt like, for a moment, the car was actually flying for a second or two.

I think the tires didn't touch the ground before descending.

All of Sam's children screamed. We loved it! It reminded us of the rollercoaster we were getting ready to ride.

One child says to the other, "I smell apples." The other child says, "I do too!" We knew that that meant. Christmas is near. Santa Clause is coming soon. Wow! Anticipation and excitement starts to build.

Like other small children, Sam's children did not know that their Poppa was also their Santa. They did not know yet that once a year, Poppa bought them the big red delicious apples, oranges and candy big bags of candy that make you know its Christmas and hid our Christmas goodies in his old wooden padlocked chest that he kept hidden in his bedroom closet.

A chest, it seems like it's been around since the beginning of time. Sometimes, when Poppa and Momma wasn't around some of his children would sneak into their parents bedroom, open the closet and stare at this old chest. A chest that held so many secrets. Sam's children wonder what they were. There were a mystery about this old chest.

As Sam's children grew older and learn that Poppa was there "Santa". Everything that was important to Poppa was kept there. That's why our "Santa" kept our Christmas gifts there.

Poppa said that his Grandpa John made this chest in the late 1800's. Gave it to his Dad, Grandpa Wesley and Grandpa Wesley gave it to him.

Sam's children like children today made their Christmas list. But our lists consisted of one gift each. And we were filled with joy with that one gift. One child wanted a comb, brush and mirror set. She got it. Another wanted a tea set. She got it.

A doll. She got it. One of the boys wanted a B.B. gun, another boy wanted a cap pistol. With these gifts we were as happy as the children today who get many gifts at Christmas.

Birthdays wasn't celebrated in the Gathing household.

On our birth days someone, it might be one of our sibling or Momma in a playful manor you'll get as many licks as your age.

Rev Gathing children wasn't allowed to listen to worldly music in his home. The Blues, Swing or R&B was not expectable. Because his children wasn't allowed to sing worldly music they turn their attention to spiritual songs. With a gang of 14 children and two nephews you could always hear church music and songs high rhythm, sweet melodies, clapping hands and stumping feet. And sometime shouting as they song to their Poppa, Momma and each other. With window wild open music and songs would vibrate and could be heard at a distant. Some of the area children said they used to sit on the road side near by so they could hear Rev Gathing children singing.

Chapter 7 - Feeling Like A Winner

Joe Louis was the World Heavyweight Boxing Champion from 1937-1949. Nicknamed the Brown Bomber, Louis helped elevate boxing by being an honest, hardworking fighter. Louis was named the greatest heavyweight of all time by the International Boxing Research Organization.

Louis's cultural impact was felt well outside the ring. He is widely regarded as the first African American to achieve the status of a nationwide hero within the United States.

June 22, 1938 between Joe Louis and Max Schmeling, the fight was held in Yankee Stadium before a crowd of 70,043.

It was broadcast by radio to million of listeners throughout the world.

Each time Joe Louis won a fight in those depression years, even before he became champion, thousand of colored American would throng out in to the streets all across the land to march and cheer and yell and cry because of Joe Louis's one man triumphs. No one else in the United States has ever had such an effect on negro emotion – or on Sam Gathing.

Why Poppa would invite friends and family over. Momma would make home made ice cream and bake a cake for the huge Joe Louis's fight. I guess you could say Poppa had one of the first "superbowl" party while they huddle around his huge battery operated radio hollering, stomping their feet just like the Super Bowl parties today.

By Joe Louis boxing with a white man in these segregated years added to the excitement.

Joe Louis hit Max Schmeling with a right and than a left.

And as these men continue to huddled around the radio each man in his own way acted out what they heard the announcer were saying.

Joe Louis, jabbed him in the chest! Oh, my! A blow to the head. Uppercut to the chin – He's out! Max Schmeling is out!

The fight last two minutes and four seconds.

Everyone busted into indescribable excitement and emotions. For Joe Louis, a black man to knock-out a big white man against the back drop of all the racial stereotype of the black man… men and women, even children, have been slain for no other earthly reason than their blackness. It was like every black man in the world had finally kicked the white man "ASS"!

Chapter 8 - They Will Kill You

There're lots of motivational books that's has been written.
How to do this How to do that. How to be happy. How not to.

But Sam had one motivational book and it was his bible.

The Bible is the truth. Poppa knew that reading his Bible that the book of truth would lead him onto all truth.

Dr. Martin L. King Jr. were lead into these truth through reading these truth. No man should be a slave to another man or a second class citizen.

Rev Gathing, like many people believed the truth. However, their surrounding culture couldn't except this truth. That all men were created in the image of God. Jesus said to love one another.

Its impossible to understand that the whites that passed the Jim Crow Law in 1857 that stated that "Negros had no rights that a white had to respect". That these whites read the same Bible that the Negros read. They read the truths in their schools, churches and home. But they didn't believe these truths. Many people died because of their unbelief.

Even under these circumstances there were many whites who took a stand with the Negros. The Quakers and John Brown comes to mind. Surrounded by thongs of hatred, like flowers on a cactus they took a stand. And some died because of it. And Negros shouldn't ignore these powerful acts of love.

John Brown a Hero for Blacks - May 9, 1800-Dec 2, 1859

John Brown an American abolitionist who advocated and practiced armed insurrection as a means to end slavery.

His attempt in 1859 to start a liberation movement among enslaved African Americans.

Brown demanded violent action in response to southern aggression.

During the Kansas campaign he and his supporters killed five proslavery southerners in what became known as the Pottawatomie Massacre in May 1856.

During the raid he led on the federal armory at Harpers Ferry, Virginia he seized the armory. Seven people including a free black were killed. Brown, intended to arm slaves with weapons from the arsenal, but the attack failed.

Brown was hang after his attempt to start a slave rebellion failed.

In behalf of the poor and the oppressed John Brown believed in the divine authenticity of the Bible.

The "Quakers" gave the runner away slaves support by putting candles in their windows to let the slaves know they could come to their house for food and shelter as the slaves were fleeing the south on their way up north or to Canada where they were seeking freedom.

The civil right struggle had escalated in the early sixties.

Preaching and the pastor of several churches kept Rev Gathing in the center of the events surrounding his environment. His awareness was always at its highest peak living under the Jim Crow Laws. The fear for his family, especially for his boys, and his people were always present. These were times of lynching and in the most feared part of Mississippi. A tough state that was ran by the Ku Klux Klan. Black people had no protection – the law wasn't on their side. The fear of lynching in the south, the threat was always there.

Rev Gathing was deeply effect by what he saw on television.

This negro man knew first hand the danger Dr King and his followers were facing. The nightly news brought the horrific struggle into everybody living room. When peaceful people came face to face with the evil dark forces of racism. These two energies clashed in a horrible force of violent.

There was bombing, attack dogs, fire hoses on small children. Killing innocent people.

Sam knew the violent the racist white could create. The terrorist Klans was a perfect example of the evil one man could create on another man. For Rev Gathing personal knew of someone who had been lynched or someone's son's body was found flowing down a river. Some of Rev Gathing members would come to him for prayer. "Our boy has been killed. The Klan did it, Rev."

Rev Gathing didn't have an answer he feared for his five boys himself. It always seem that it was the boys. The Negro young men the racist white men wanted to destroy.

And now in the twenth century so many of our black boys are destroying themselves.

After counseling his members Rev Gathing would tell them to prayer. To ask God for mercy. That what he did himself.

Why it was a crime that was so shameful; filled with repugnance and fear. One of Sam's boys had been raped by some of the Klansmen. Poppa told his boys don't tell anyone especially his younger children so this hideous crime was whispered about for years.

He tried to push this horrible crime against his oldest son out of his mind. Maybe if he didn't think about it this nightmare would go away. But of course it didn't. Whenever our Poppa read or heard or saw horror on T.V., this hideous crime would come rushing back to his memory as though it had just happened.

To know that these evil men was free to go on with their lives as though nothing had happened; for them to attend their Sunday church services and enjoy their family, Rev. Gathing knew who they were. In these small towns everyone knew who did what and what they did. The irony of it all, sometimes people with authority was involved in these hate crimes.

Sometimes while driving, our Poppa would see these men in their pick-up trucks driving in the opposite direction.

"Those are the men that raped my son. That's them alright!" Poppa said out loud.

He prayed for the ability to function in his day-to-day routine because sometimes this cross was too heavy to carry.

He felt so helpless. He couldn't undo what was wrong by retaliating because he knew he couldn't find justice in the court of law.

Sam and Beatrice teenage son, Junior, that's what they called him. The anger and rage this young boy felt for these evil men emerged into hostility toward all white men. He saw them all as "blue-eyed devils". Junior also struggle with who am I really? What was a real black man suppose to be like?

Rev. Gathing son spent time in the military. His time spent servicing in South Korea in the middle 50's added to his confusion and anger.

(r) Junior

Our brother like most young recruits had never set foot on foreign soil. For this huge cargo plane was his first flight. So when these young soldiers, after a 20 hour flight, disembarked in Seoul, South Korea, the culture shock was hard to express in words. There was even an unfamiliar smell in the air.

This strange environment had millions and millions of people. Junior had never seen this many people before. They were yellowed skinned with jet black hair. Even their eyes were different. The men wore dark suites, white shirts and neckties. Their black shoes were spotless. The women had on straight dark jackets.

Poppa oldest son noticed right away that the men and the women too were taking every step with pride and confidence. Is this what real men was suppose to look like?

He was thinking.

He watched them as they walked with their family, as their children went to school. He was amazed to see groups of people doing their exercise in the public square. Here in this strange environment thousands of miles away from America was the first time he didn't feel threatened. Junior didn't feel danger or harm.

The only men he had ever seen who controlled their environment were the American white male. The Koreans did everything in order. Within a short time, these strangers became his heroes.

Junior walked the path of anger and unforgiveness calling Mohammed his "God". All power to Elijah Mohammed. All praises to ALLAH. This was his praises until the very end of his life that cancer took the summer of 2010 at the age of 78. On his deathbed he forgave those evil men who long ago on that dirt road on a warm Mississippi night while he was rushing home to Momma because he knew Momma worried about her boys while they were out at night. It only took these wicked men a few minutes to rob him of his joy and inner peace.

The evil that men do lives after them - William Shakespeare

As Junior laid dying, he called out to the God of his Poppa, Jesus! Jesus, have mercy on me. The prayers of his Momma and Poppa brought him through.

So, as our Poppa watched the horror of the images of the Civil right movement, the Freedom Rider, Dr King speaking out in a strong voice. "We hold these truths to be self evident that a people has the right to the pursue of happiness. Some truth is God given.

Dr King and his follower stood so close to this evil they even rubbed the racist white spit off their faces. King and his followers stood their ground. Unyielding they stood. Attack dogs, high pressure water hoses. They stood. Police bully clubs. They stood unyielding. Singing their freedom songs "We shall over come."

What Rev Gathing and other were watching on television And throughout the world was hard to believe. Words that Were whispered in their mouth, talked about in their homes.

Secret words about those "white folks". Because to speak them openly would cause death to you or one of your boys.

Lynching, burning being dragged with a rope tied behind a truck while a white driver and his buddies inside laughing and telling nigger jokes.

Sam knew the evil of these southern whites. He lived his life while in the midst of their horror.

So when Poppa said to his family and to God as he watched Dr King on T.V. "Lord have mercy, they're going to kill that man.

Rev Gathing knew what he was talking about.

Dr King and his followers knew that Americans had not lived up to its promises… America had to face the lies they were telling the world. Foreign countries thought all of American citizens were free. As late as the sixty they were not.

Chapter 9 - The Mourner's Bench

Typically when a child enters the beginning of his or her teens, church members put focus on him or her because this is the age when a child usually begins to feel a draw by the Holy Spirit. And recognizes that he or her must seek salvation from sin. However, a person can feel this draw at a much younger or older age. Once a year the church would do a revival service. Members meet nightly for a week. The church believed that a young person must be drawn by the Holy Spirit to seek God. That (1 Tim. 3:8-13) salvation isn't automatic.

The children that the Holy Spirit called would all sit on the front bench a Bench that's called the "Mourner Bench" The Pastor, Deacons and the whole church would sing, pray and shout after the Preacher had finished preaching about little children come to Jesus. Jesus love the little children.

Come children give your heart to Jesus. Reaching out his hands "Won't you come? Jesus is waiting, please come. You don't want to be lost in Hell's eternal fire where there will be burning and gnashing of teeth.

Many old people came and knelt also standing as they song while clapping their hands spiritual songs of joy.

I got rid of my heavy load.
Somebody got rid of there heavy load on Monday.
Somebody stand up today and say they got rid of their
heavy load.
On a Tuesday I got rid of my heavy load.

Or

Come on mourner in the army of the Lord
You've to die in the army of the Lord.

As the singing, and praying continue one or more of the mourners would begin to shout signifying that they had received the Holy Spirit. The whole church would rejoice with them shouting and praising the Lord that a soul had been saved. And when the new convert had finished shouting they would be placed near the altar meaning they have come to Jesus. This ritual would continue for a week.

Baptism

After a week of revival services Rev Gathing took his new converts down to the river to be baptized. The water was cold. It chilled their bodies but not their souls; in the name of the Father, the Son & the Holy Spirit I baptize you. As Rev Gathing and his deacons immerse each new convert into the cold waist deep water.

Sometimes Rev Gathing would baptize one of his own children. How did Rev Gathing feel when he immerse one of his own – in the name of the Father the Son and the Holy Spirit.

Rev Gathing felt the anointing going through him to his own child. And he prayed that all the new converts would receive the anointing praying also that the seed that was planted in this river of cold water would fall on fertile ground.

Looking back to the mourner's era in the year of 2010 it may seem foolish now… was all that necessary? You may ask.

You decide. Today's youth, thank God not all of them, the satanic rap music, low-slung style pants that hangs below the butt and underwear for all to see, these kids are blocking the light form their grandparents generations.

They, especially the teenage black boys are bring in so much darkness that the hope and prayers through their grandparent's struggle has been weakened. They've given the civil right movement a black eye.

What happen to them? Many are asking.

A generational curse. Maybe. The breakdown of the Afro American family were deeply effected by the growth of the black male in the prison population.

It is true that there's extremely high violent in the black male population.

However theirs is always unseen story behind what we witness. It's always more to it than we think…

His heart was filled with anger against his black brother onto the point of threats of death by shooting. Some middle age men would rush and get their pistol speed off in their automobile to wave their pistol in another black man face… if you don't pay me the money you own me I'll shoot you M_ _ _ _ _!

Most of the time this angry out burst was just a threat.

Just to get their attention. However, their teenager sons heard their dads or another angry black man say these offer angry words filled with extreme hostility. These boys took it to the next lowest level and actual pulled the trigger killing their perceived enemy that look like him self.

It may not be acceptable to talk about it. Sometimes they don't believe the facts. The facts, however, unpleasant they are and they include the high murder rate in our young black male population. Its obvious the threats these young men hears dismantle their love they should have for their brothers.

The melodrama of it all. "It all happen so suddenly. The mother amiss sobs and tears says what happen? My baby were here yesterday today I'm at the morgue."

There is, though, enough black males and females in college which gives us a ray of light, a ray of hope. It also shows us too that our grandparents prayers hasn't totally been lost. That some seeds that was planted generations ago fell on fertile ground. By all of this we are encouraged.

In the middle 1800's blacks were force into independent.

During this time in our history the impoverished black communities made large contributions to the first black schools. 1865; Fisk, Lincoln, 1866 Talladega, Howard, Morehouse and there were many other. Their remembrance of slavery were fresh in their minds. The negro men and women didn't take their freedom for granted. The promise of "Forty acres and a mule" didn't happen. Blacks learned a hard lessons. Whites were not going to do it for them. So they buckled down and did it for themselves.

During this segregation era there were 83 private schools that were started by and ran by Negroes where Negroes could pay for a high school education in Mississippi because there was no public school for black s that went beyond the ninth grade.

The Baptist Industrial Academy also known as B.I, in Hernando, MS., was one of those schools (1887-1957).

B.I., in fact was the only place in Desoto County, MS. that Negroes could pay for a high school education.

These children came from all over the county in search for a high school education. Most parents was following the teaching of Booker T. Washington (up from slavery).

"If the Negroes were to succeed in America, they must be educated."

Rev. Gathing was in the midst of this zeal for education.

He sent his oldest son, Junior, his two daughters, Ruth and Cozetta, to B.I. and his younger children were looking forward to going also.

To be away from home, out of the watchful eyes of our parents was more than Sam and Beatrice younger children could hope for and to live in a dormitory; to share a room like Ruth and Cozetta. Wow! When we visited our sisters in Hernando, MS., with excitement, we saw a glimpse into what we anticipated our future would look like.

Poppa said he read somewhere, "if you think education is expensive, you should consider the cost of being ignorant".

In 1954 U.S. Supreme Court declared segregated school unconstitutional in the Brown v Board of Education. When public high school open for Negro kids it threw these black private school into confusion and chaos. For the first time in Negro's history, Negroes didn't have to pay for a high school education and colored citizens took advantage of this change by sending their children to public schools. One by one, these private schools started closing because the demands were no longer there.

Chapter 10 - Renting No More

Exodus 13:14 – with a mighty hand the Lord brought us out of Egypt, out of the land of slavery.
God brought Sam out of Egypt. Egypt a land of renting.

A land where the racist white men ruled.

He knew his bible and it had shaped his own world view.

Sam personalized the concept of God. Knowing these words were TRUTH. He read in his bible about the struggle Moses had bring the Israelites out of bondage in Egypt. Renting land from racist land owners and having to obey them, he recognized he and his family were living in bondage. He had a deep longing for more.

In 1954 the greatest milestone of their 25 years marriage and 14 children later, they signed the final papers on their 150 acres of land. The $4,000.00 they needed hadn't come easy.

It took years of hard labor to arrive at this blessed moment.

With the echo of nigger, do this, nigger go there, come here nigger these days were behind him now.

With his wife by his side Sam signed the final papers.

Did his hands tremble? How could it not.

"That something you call dirt is something" Sam told his children" Lord, this land is something. Once you own it they can't take it away.

It's hard to imagine the joy Sam and his wife felt when they first set foot on their own land. Did he stoop down and get a hand full of their soil so that he and Beatrice could smell the richness of their land? He, from reading his bible knew what a miracle was. And this was a miracle. Now was the time to praise God. And that night before going to bed Sam and Beatrice knelt down on their knees while holding hands and gave God, the praise, thanks and the glory.

Sam and Beatrice Gathing

Chapter 11 - "Momma"

I've stated this before I think it bares repeating here. During the time of the Jim Crow Laws, blacks and whites in the South were forced into separation. Separate school, separate neighborhoods separate public eating placing. Whites had school buses. Negro kids in the 1950's didn't have school buses in Mississippi. Our books was left over used books that the white school didn't want anymore.

Beatrice children would rush home from school with the smell of a pot of pinto beans and ham hocks cooking or maybe cabbage and corn bread waiting for their hungry stomach maybe some home made tea cakes or fried apple pies and tell her about the insults they encounter from the white children as the bus load of white kids past them while they were walking from school, "Hey you stupid nigger"! The Nigger kids has to walk" Sometimes some of the white kids while leaning with head sticking through the bus window with sneering, contemptuous facial express would spit on us.

And as the big yellow school bus past us with the Mississippi red dust from the gravel road covering us we could hear laughter from the white children. Ha! Hah!! Ha, ha!

How do you think Beatrice felt listening to her kids telling her about the insults they've encounter – how can she fight against a system that was design to bully her children. How can she prevent them from turning bitter? For earlier that day, Momma had gone to her vegetable garden and picked fresh vegetable for her family and during midsummer there was an abundant supply. This time of the year Momma's garden was overflowing with ripe fruits and vegetables. Our mother and her older daughters assisted her in canning part of the surplus vegetable for future use. Poppa and his older boys, likewise, would slaughter a hog and momma would, after making sausages, preserve some of these in glass jars also. Beatrice looked at her children. Momma, looked at her children as they were eating. They looked the same no frowns on their faces except, maybe, they wasn't smiling as much. You know how children are they always seem to shake everything off so easily. As she watch them eating she said a silently prayer for her children that that incident of extreme verbal hatred thrown at her children almost on a daily bases as they walked to school wouldn't destroy their spirit; for everyone had heard about that Till boy – Emmett Till was his name. Why they killed that boy. The K.K.K. did it, alright. I heard somewhere that that poor fourteen – year – old boy before his mother put him on the bus leaving Chicago to see him off to spend two week vacation with his relatives in Mississippi Delta. His mother did the same thing me and Sam always do down here in Mississippi. We tell our children how to act and talk around them white folks. There are rules down here we color folks has to live by because if you don't you'll die.

Mommas and Poppas all through the south teach their kids on a daily bases what they must 1. Always say "Yes sir and No Sir" 2. Never look them in the eyes because they'll think you are an uppity nigger. White folks don't like uppity niggers. They have been known to be lynched. We also tell our children especially our boys if they tell you to "kneel down" do it. Because child, whites has no law or rules that they have to obey regarding Negros. But we have to obey them as they make or change their minds about Negros.

You know that Till boy made head line news when they lynched that boy for looking at that white girl. But no one is talking about brother Franklin son, that deacon in our church. The dogs found his boy near the river. They found him dead with his face down in the mud.

"Lord have mercy", was our Momma daily prayer. In Sunday school we teach our children to love one another. Lord, Momma thinking to herself how can I Lord teach my kids to love these evil white folk. Lord, Jesus I know its some good whites. But down here in Mississippi they are so mean. Lord, only you Jesus know the reason they are the way they are.

This was the prayers of the faithful, who had never ceased, both day and night, to cry out for deliverance. Momma and Poppa read in their bible that they would be delivered out of this horrible fear of raising their kids here. How long before one of her five boys react in respond to their hostile environment.

That's the way Momma felt a few years later when her youngest son James went to Vietnam. She heard about the hand grenades, mind fields. All that shooting, danger all around. Why her baby boy was in the midst of it all. It was awful. We could hear Momma praying. Why some times as we walked past her and Poppa cracked bedroom door we could get a glimpse of Momma on her knees kneeled in prayer. Momma felt that way, not quite as bad, but sort of that way when one of her boys left the house. Praying they would follow the rules set for the Negros.

Why she could see the times were changing. Negros in the South was stirring up lots of trouble listening to Dr. King, Malcolm X, the Black Panther. Momma said "these men are going to get my boys killed."

Once Beatrice family were safely in her home, none of her boys were out in the night where the threat of impending danger or harm was a real menace; there was laughter.

Momma children would keep her laughing. We use to love to touch her on her sides. With a light touch our mother would jump. We knew she was so "ticklish".

Even not sparing the rod "our home was filled with laughter. When Momma whipped us with a belt or a switch which she sometime would tell us to go and get a switch from that elm tree out back… Now that was hard to do – to pick out a long twig from this tree Momma would choose between the switch from this tree and a belt.

This may sound strange but as soon as the pain from the whipping had stopped in a little while we were playful again.

Momma children knew that the bible said to "spare the rod ruin the child

"What am I going to cook today" Momma said I'm so tired of cooking. Three times a day Momma cooked.

Breakfast, dinner and supper. Momma never took a vacation.

Disciplining, nursing, teaching etc.

But, she saw her life changing. Her children had started feeling maybe these white folks were right about them – ugly nappy headed nigger kids. Black and ugly. Dumb, stupid nigger kids. Why, now Beatrice heard her children call themselves those horrible names. One of her children would say to the other "you got nigger hair and you are black and ugly". For she and Sam couldn't protect them from their surrounding. The negative influence was devastating on her family. Momma would say "my children ain't ugly".

Then, it seem out of nowhere – through the radio" I am black and I am proud. Black is beautiful. Her children started singing a new song. She and their father had told their children not to listen to worldly music. Evil music. But this music was difference. It seem like it was coming not from the world but these songs were God sent. This worldly man James Brown was sing I'm black and am proud. Lord have mercy. Momma felt Joy. Now her children started to believe her that maybe just maybe they're not ugly after all.

Sam and Beatrice children had begun the process of breaking away from the psychological barrier of fear which had imprisoned blacks in the past. They were rapidly fleeing from Mississippi. Because they felt trapped there. The fence that was placed around them were too narrow. Her children couldn't grow. Their father had a tight reign on his daughters.

Jim Crow Laws were literally chocking them. Interfering with their mental growth. They heard about the opportunities up North. And that's where they wanted to be.

Momma wanted to clutch, hang on to her children as they took off. Leaving her. It was so hard on our mother. And with all of this, Momma knew that something wasn't right with her. Momma told her husband "things just go out of my mind. When I try to explain I can't say what I want to say".

Momma was scared. Sam started seeing a gradually change in his wife. Our Poppa told his children its something wrong with "Brassy". Your mother isn't herself anymore. She forget stuff.

When Momma was diagnosed with Alzheimer's disease in the early sixty Poppa was scared too. He was a man who always had great demands on his time. His family, his churches. His farm. However, though, when his wife of 57 years go sick he took care of her until his death in 1986.

After Poppa's death, Cozetta, Momma's third child couldn't bare the thought of putting our beloved mother in a nursing home that was used as a dumping ground for the old unwanted people. The thought was too depressing for her. The image of nursing home kept running through her mind. Old people lined a long the corridor. Some in wheel chairs, some with hands gripping walkers to support them as they shuffle along. Lonely old people - Sharing a room with a stranger. Eating food they didn't like.

It was a decision that she had to make. Night after night Momma was on Cozetta's mind. Lying in her bed beside her husband in a Chicago suburban middle class neighborhood a mother of four. Cozetta was content with her life, content with being a wife and mother, running her and her husband small business. The store of antiques and used furniture.

She loved doing what she was doing. She loved talking with her customers. Looked forward to going to her church on Sunday…

But Momma, the woman that nursed her babies, gave them the home remedies that was passed down from generations to generation, when her children were sick, made and mended their clothes when they needed mending. This was often, for you see back then, poor people didn't buy their children clothes until the old clothes were worn out. One pair of shoes.

So the need for our mother to sew on button, sew on patches, to mend ripped cloths was always there. "Child come and thread this needle, for your young eyes are better than mine", Momma would say.

Cozetta, remember so clearly Momma giving birth to her younger siblings at home. Natural childbirth we call it today.

But back then in the 30's – 50's Momma was just having another baby. Cynthia, Cozetta and even little Ruth could hear the agony pangs and intense struggle of their mother in labor.

It was easy for Beatrice's children to hear what was going on in this old framed shack. The walls was thin for if they could search they may find a crack and peek and see what that midwife woman was doing to their Momma.

It seems to Cozetta's 6 years old mind like it took hours and hours even maybe a whole day before they finally heard the cry of their new baby. Cozetta, remember Momma being so tired Cozetta, remember too, how Momma and her sisters would sometimes get together all nine of the Bowen girls talking quietly when there were no men or children around. They would tell her little secrets about how not to get pregnant.

So often, when Beatrice girls were old enough to understand, Momma would share these same secrets with her girls. During these times there were no legal birth control for women.

Momma, it seem to her sisters, that she was always pregnant. Our mother and Poppa thought that children came from God. So with this in mind Momma gave birth to fifteen babies.

The Bowen girl were pretty, fiery women full of life and fancy as they puffed on their cigarettes. Beatrice didn't smoke.

Momma girls wanted to be like their aunts. Wow! We thought they were so cool.

They all had shoulder length hair – with their light brown skin. Their dresses were just below their knees with shapely legs accenting their pretty high heel shoes.

Pauline (Bowen) Bridgeford
(Beatrice Sister)

Our sister knew Momma couldn't take the kind of change that a nursing home would require. And Cozetta couldn't stand the thought of her "sweet pea" living with the indignities of a nursing home. She knew she had to leave the comfort of her life style and after talking with her family, especially her husband, Clem who gave her his blessing. Cozetta went down to Mississippi, after closing their small business and brought our mother to live with her and her family.

As Momma laid in her hospital bed in Cozetta's and Clem's sunny bright family room the wall has series of rows of family pictures reaching back and forward over several generations.

A visiting nurse came through the week to assist Cozetta and show her how to care for a hospice patient. Our sister did what she'd been doing daily for the past three years. After adjusting the feeding tube and with a soft damp warm face cloth she would wash her mother's hands and face gently. As usual, Momma would go to sleep. Cozetta, stood looking down at her "sweet pea" for a few moments thinking to herself how peaceful and beautiful she looked making sure Momma was comfortable. Before she started to go back up stairs, Cozetta picked up her basket of freshly washed folded clothes and headed up stairs. As Cozetta was climbing the stairs she heard the Holy Spirit so clearly "Your mother is dead".

She turned so quickly dropping the basket of freshly folded clothes and running back down the stairs to her dead mother she almost tripped. With uncontrollable weeping and trembling hands she dialed 911. She's dead my mother is dead.

Momma's home remedies
1. A teaspoon of flour – for diarrhea.
2. Gargle with warm salty water for sore throat.
3. Check temperature – a slight touch on the forehead or the side of the neck.
4. Epsom salt for upset stomach.
5. Baking soda for brushing teeth and for deodorant.
6. 1 – teaspoon of sugar with 1 or 2 drops of turpentine for digestive track worms.

7. Vick's Vapor Rub for stuffy nose.
8. Cold sores – a little ear wax.
9. Corn Husks tea – for bed wetting.

This bedtime prayer was required of the Gathing children.
Now I lay me down to sleep
I pray to the Lord my soul to keep
If I should die before I awake
I pray to God my soul He shall take
Bless Momma, Poppa and everybody
Amen.

"Momma" age approx. 46

Roberta at The Great Wall of China - Beijing 1999

Church of the Holy Sepulchre - Jerusalem, Israel 1988

Egypt - Ramses II - Roberta in Egypt 1988

Roberta with a Masai Tribe, Kenya Africa - 1992

Roberta with Africa Village in Senegal Africa - 2000

Chapter 12 - Epilogue

Scripture from the bible has been mentioned many times throughout this book. This Epilogue will show the anger and rebellion of young people who felt they were wiser than their parents.

I like my siblings, especially by brothers, were caught up in "power to the people", "we want it now", era. Angela Davis, Malcolm X was some of my heroes too.

A few weeks after high school graduation, my twin sister, Alberta and I packed all of our belongings - one suitcase. We caught the Greyhound Bus to live with our sister Ruth and her family in North St. Louis, MO.

As the bus took us through Arkansas and Missouri, with nervousness and excitement, our eyes were glued to the scenery passing outside the bus window because at the age of 18, we hadn't seen the world outside of Mississippi and Tennessee.

With anger and resentment still burning within us, the way our family, especially our Poppa was treated, the more distant we put between us and Mississippi, the better. We hated Mississippi, the Jim Crow Laws, the work in the fields, the awful Mississippi heat, all the worms and insects that goes with it!

The Land that No One Wanted

The land that Poppa paid such a high emotional price for, his children didn't want. We rejected the land its people. This illustrates what damage resentment can do.

By rejecting our inheritance, it seem as though we were affected by some type of "mental virus".

Jim Crow Laws had gain a stronghold on Rev. Gathing children. His children rejected the white ruling class and the land that was stained by generations of our people's blood.

This influence gain dominance in our soulish realm where the mind, will and emotions are located and they began to control that individual and consequently, his future generation. (Hickey)

Perhaps even worse, no matter how we tried, living in the midst of the white ruling class, we felt inferior it seem to that the lighter the complexion of the woman, the closer the black women skin color were to the white woman the more our black men were attracted to them. This rejection was deeply felt especially when we looked at our black men we felt in our heart. "The blacker the berry the sweeter the juice" or "we don't want no cream in our coffee".

We tried hard not to see our blackness as ugly and undesirable. Straightening our kinky hair and using bleaching cream on our face didn't improve our self-perception. The psychological consequence from this rejection has been huge.

Leaving Mississippi didn't stop my desire to leave America where I believed this country was the cause of the Negro's problems. Like so many others, myself included, was blinded by my resentment for America which caused me to ignore all the blessings and the people who had sacrificed so much for me to receive those blessings.

During my "militant" years, wearing my large afro, If there was a protest, I was in the midst of the crowd holding my protest sign high so that others could see..."Down with America!"

I even toyed with the idea of changing my name."Who wants to hang on to the names of their slave masters?" I asked. Influences of Malcolm X.

Sometimes I would visit Moslem Mosque which through me into a spiritual identity crisis.

Reading other people history, traveling to developing countries, especially Africa, standing in the Doors of No Return, where the slaves passed through the doors to be forced to America. I wept for my ancestors. I also witnessed abject poverty. In Egypt, I guess seeing the ruins of antiquity and standing on the great wall of China, changed my ungrateful attitude about America. Getting out of the forest I definitely could see the trees.

I've heard it said, "When you don't know what you're looking at, you don't know what you see". Don't allow yourself to hold on to resentment and unforgiveness. If you do, you will never be free.

As I write this book, I am a senior citizen. The God I service is the God of my father.

The scriptures I quote daily are the same scriptures Poppa quoted.

Remembering Junior...

His experiences with the southern whites filled his conscious with anger and resentment. Even in his anger, Junior never forgot to remember his younger sisters and brothers. When he would come home, we would rush to meet him so we could receive the candy and gum we knew he had in his pockets for us.

Junior was into body building. Being a real man was his thing. He had big strong muscles. He displayed his physique with pride. We enjoyed watching him flexing and posing his masculine physique.

As young children, he would lift one of us up by his bicep to show us how strong he was. Sometimes we would watch him as he told us to count how many push-ups he could do or "come sit on my back" he would tell one of us. I'll show you how many I can do even while you are on my back.

Junior was very upset when society, the people and government wasn't responding the way he thought they should have to current events.

As should be expected, as he got older he was angry and frustrated most of the time.

Jackie's life with her dad was an extremely difficult one-passing through many toils and snares. His belief in Mohammed, her belief in Jesus Christ - this drew a strong dividing line in their relationship.

In spite of the fact that their was a line drawn in their relationship, she never stopped honoring him as her father.

Even if he was confused about who he was. For this was what she believed "that her dad was a child of God".

Jackie, sometimes under and against great odds, always with patience in his final days, she took care of her dad in her home with her and her family.

As she prayed for her dying father, she also asked her church, her aunts and her cousins. Anyone who prayed, she would ask them to pray for her dad. With sobbing and weeping, "I don't want Satan to take my dad", she said.

Although Junior was a fighter at the end he had to completely surrender to cancer.

Upon one of my visits to see my dying brother in Memphis, TN, and as Jackie and one of Junior's grandchildren would assist their mother in lifting their granddad's frail body, the love I witnessed moved me to tears.

Chapter 13 - About the Author

Roberta was born Roberta Gathing the 10th of Beatrice and Sam's fourteen children in 1943 into Jim Crow Laws in Northern Mississippi.

She writes about how difficult it was to watch their father having to act like a "boy" and being called a "boy" by the southern whites.

Even though Rev. Gathing pastor four churches and was the moderator Sardis East Baptist B the confederation didn't change whites' way of addressing him as "boy".

Roberta, like her father, appreciated reading and travel.

The many books she read and the series of countries she's visited reflects that. This includes Africa, Asia, China, Egypt, Israel and South America.

Roberta left Mississippi after graduating from high school to live with her sister Ruth, her husband and their three small children in a 2nd story three room apartment in North St. Louis, City (MO).

She retired from Mallinckrodt Chemical after 37 years.

During this time she also sold real estate and owned a small ice cream parlor which, her daughter, Pam managed for her.

Chapter 14 - Gathing Family Tree

William "Grandpa Bill" Gathing, born March 1828 in Anson County N. Carolina, died March 20, 1017 in Lewisburg, MS.

William first union was to Isabella Arrington, Born 1845 in Campbell County, Virginia, died 1897 Lewisburg, MS.

From this union 8 children were born: Julia 1861, Fannie 1862, Mary 1866/died 1909, Kizzie 1872, Elizabeth 1872/ died 1909, Willie 1877, Henry 1879 and Eugenia 1882.

William was married again, Susie Collins, and from that union were John Wesley(Sr.), December 1857/died 1924 and Mattie born June 6, 1867/died April 23 1951.

William also married Sallie, born May 1855. To this union were 3 sons, Peter, March 1887; Taylor Olanoh, May 1882; Andrew, June 1891 and 1 daughter, Perola, February 1887.

John Wesley Sr. was married to Mollie (Dasher), born April 1869. From this union were 5 sons John Wesley Jr., May 1880; Cary L, Oct 1881; Dave, June 1882; Lucious, 1889 and Hilliard (adopted); and 4 daughters, Cora & Dora, February 1885 and Jessie, August 1893 and Georgia.

John Wesley Jr. married January 2, 1904 to *Cynthia Nesbit, born May 1884. From this union 2 children were born, Mary, 1906 and Samuel Wesley, April 25, 1908 and Lilly Bowen, born 1889. Cynthia died approximately six-months after Samuel was born.

John Wesley Jr. married **Millie Bowen and from this union were 2 sons, Emerson, 1911 and Booker T, 1912.

John Wesley married a 3rd time to Etta; also known as Mae Ella Baker or Big Momma and from this union Iola was born in 1915.

*Simon Nesbit, born 1848, married May 17, 1880, Mary Spencer, date of birth unknown. From this union were 6 children, William, Mary, Charles, Jerry born Feb 1883 (married Lena; daughter Gillie born Oct 1896), Cynthia, born May 1884, and Lilly, born 1886.

**Millie Bowen was the aunt of Beatrice Bowen, wife of Samuel Wesley Gathing.

Samuel Wesley and Beatrice were married December 22, 1929 and from this union there were 14 children:

Cynthia, Samuel Wesley Jr. (died 2010), Obadiah, Cozetta, Ruth, Christine, Alfred, Iola (died 2004), Alberta, Roberta, Lloyd, James, Betty Jo and Peggy.

****

The author is indebted to the following:

- James Mabley for the material on the family tree
- Corrine Davis on the history of Mt. Sinai Church
- Elnora Jackson on the information on Pastor Royer Person
- Marilyn Hickey, "Breaking Generational Curses"
- My sister Ruth Wilson for the information on B.I
- John Brown "Stephen B. Oats: To Purge This Land with Blood"
- Phillip Dray, "At The Hands of Persons Unknown - The Lynching of Black America"
- Langston Hughes, "The Mourner's Bench", "Salvation"

Excerpts from World Wide Web:
- ABC News, "Baggy Pants"
- "Joe Louis's Greatest Fight: Louis Schemling"